OTHER YOUNG YEARLING BOOKS YOU WILL ENJOY:

CORNSTALKS AND CANNONBALLS, *Barbara Mitchell*
THE TOWN THAT MOVED, *Mary Jane Finsand*
HELEN KELLER—CRUSADER FOR THE BLIND
AND DEAF, *Stewart and Polly Anne Graff*
GEORGE WASHINGTON CARVER AGRICULTURAL SCIENTIST,
*Sam and Beryl Epstein*
LEO AND EMILY, *Franz Brandenberg*
LEO AND EMILY AND THE DRAGON, *Franz Brandenberg*
LEO AND EMILY'S BIG IDEA, *Franz Brandenberg*
LEO AND EMILY'S ZOO, *Franz Brandenberg*
THE ADVENTURES OF MOLE AND TROLL, *Tony Johnston*
HAPPY BIRTHDAY, MOLE AND TROLL, *Tony Johnston*

YEARLING BOOKS/YOUNG YEARLINGS/YEARLING CLASSICS are designed especially to entertain and enlighten young people. Patricia Reilly Giff, consultant to this series, received her bachelor's degree from Marymount College and a master's degree in history from St. John's University. She holds a Professional Diploma in Reading and a Doctorate of Humane Letters from Hofstra University. She was a teacher and reading consultant for many years, and is the author of numerous books for young readers.

For a complete listing of all Yearling titles,
write to Dell Readers Service,
P.O. Box 1045, South Holland, IL 60473

DEC    1993

# Deborah Sampson Goes to War

## by Bryna Stevens
## pictures by Florence Hill

A Young Yearling Book

*To Erin Puls, who reads a lot*

Published by
Dell Publishing
a division of
Bantam Doubleday Dell Publishing Group, Inc.
666 Fifth Avenue
New York, New York 10103

ISBN: 0-440-40552-1

Reprinted by arrangement with Carolrhoda Books, Inc.

Printed in the United States of America

December 1991

10  9  8  7  6  5  4  3  2  1

CWO

# New Words

**Colonists** are people who settle in a new country but still have ties with the country they left.

A **musket** is a kind of firearm, similar to a rifle, that was used during the Revolutionary War. Muskets were 6 or 7 feet long and weighed about 40 pounds. **Musket balls** were the bullets for muskets.

**Patriots** are people who love their country and believe in it strongly. The people called **patriots** during the Revolutionary War were those who felt a stronger loyalty to America than they did to England.

A **probe** is a thin metal rod. In the days of the Revolutionary War, probes were used to remove musket balls from wounded soldiers.

In the United States, when people disagree with something, they can **protest** against it. In the 1700s, the patriots protested against English taxes by having the Boston Tea Party. Today, people still protest against taxes. They also protest against such things as nuclear power plants, nuclear weapons, and war.

A **regiment** is a large unit of soldiers in an army.

In 1760 George Washington
had been married one year.

Thomas Jefferson
was just starting college.
He was 16 years old.

Benjamin Franklin
was visiting Europe.

Mrs. Sampson was having a baby.

Deborah Sampson was born
on December 17, 1760.
During the first five years
of her life,
George Washington worried about
pleasing his wife, Martha.

Thomas Jefferson worried about getting good grades.

Benjamin Franklin worried about politics.

The Sampsons worried about money.
They never seemed to have enough.

Finally Mr. Sampson decided
to become a sailor.
Off he went to sea,
with high hopes of making
enough money to feed his family.
But his ship was lost in a storm.
His family never saw him again.
Neither did anyone else.

There were few jobs for women
in the 1760s.
Mrs. Sampson could not take care of
six children all by herself.
She sent some to live with relatives.
Deborah moved in with her cousin,
then with a pastor's widow.
Finally, when she was 10 years old,
Deborah went to live
with the Benjamin Thomas family.
This turned out to be a lucky move.
Deborah had to work hard
at the Thomases'.
She plowed fields and milked cows.
She fed animals
and made all her own clothes.
But she also got to go to school!
In 1770 not many girls were that lucky.

Deborah loved school.
She especially loved learning to read.
Soon she was reading
all the newspapers she could find.
What was she reading about?
Taxes, for one thing.
At that time the United States
was made up of 13 colonies.
It wasn't even called
the United States yet.
All those colonies belonged to Britain.
Britain needed money,
so it began to pass new laws.
These laws made the colonists
pay taxes on many things,
like newspapers and tea and paint.
The money from these taxes
went to Britain.

Many colonists didn't think
that was fair at all.
Why should their money go to Britain?
They were building a new world.
They needed their money at home!
Britain should leave them alone!
Britain should let them
govern themselves!
These angry colonists
were called patriots.
Deborah agreed with them.

In 1773 Deborah read about
the Boston Tea Party.
Some patriots had sneaked
onto 3 British ships.
They had thrown
340 chests of British tea
into the sea.
They were protesting the taxes.
Deborah felt they were right.

In 1775 Deborah read the latest news.
British soldiers and the colonists
had begun to fight.
The American Revolution had started.

Deborah wanted to fight too,
but she was only 14 years old.
Besides, she was a girl.
Only boys and men
were allowed to join the army.
But 7 years later Deborah was 21,
and the war was still going on.
Deborah was now a tall young woman.
In fact, she was taller than many men.
She was strong too.
She had plowed fields.
She was a good carpenter.
Once she had even built a barn.
"If men can fight for freedom,"
she wondered, "why can't I?"

The more she thought about it,
the more she wanted to fight.
So one day Deborah sewed a man's suit.

She tied her hair back the way men did.

She tied a cloth
tightly around her breasts
so that her chest was flat like a man's.
She put on her new suit.
Then she walked 35 miles
to Billingham, Massachusetts.
There she joined the army.

No one in Billingham knew Deborah.
She signed her name Robert Shurtleff.
No one guessed she was a woman.
Everyone thought she was a young man.
Some American soldiers
were only 16 years old.
Deborah joined a regiment
at West Point, near New York City.
In the daytime
she marched with her regiment.
In the evening
the soldiers took baths
in the Hudson River.
Deborah always took her baths
late at night.
No one found out
that she was a woman.

Fighting was hard
around New York City.
Soon Deborah's regiment
was called into action.
Deborah and some other soldiers
were sent to spy on the British.
They found out
where the British were camped.
Then they reported it.
The next day
the Americans attacked and won.

Deborah's next job
was even more dangerous.
The British were stealing cows
from American farmers.
The cows became food
for the British army.
Deborah's regiment was told
to put a stop to this stealing.

During the battle
a bullet hit Deborah's head.
Two musket balls went into her leg.
"Don't take me to a hospital,"
she begged. "Just let me die!"
Of course the soldiers
refused to obey her.
Instead, a soldier put her on his horse.
He rode six miles to a hospital.

Deborah was badly hurt,
but she was afraid of the hospital
more than she was afraid of pain.
She was sure that someone
would find out
that she was a woman.
A doctor bandaged her head.
"Do you have any other wounds?"
he asked.
"No," Deborah lied.
The doctor turned away.
Just then he noticed Deborah's pants
lying on a chair.
He picked them up.
He poked his finger through a hole
made by a musket ball.
"What's this?" he asked.

"I tore my pants on some branches,"
Deborah told him.
The doctor believed her.

Deborah didn't sleep that night.
When everyone was quiet,
she got up and found a long metal probe.
Metal probes were used
to remove musket balls.
She found some bandages too.
Deborah limped back to bed.
She pushed the probe into her leg.
She removed one musket ball.
The other stayed in her leg.
Deborah couldn't reach it.
It was in too deep.

Each day in the hospital
Deborah worried that someone
would learn her secret.
She was so worried
that she left the hospital
before she was completely well.
Luckily her next job was easy.
She went to work for General Paterson
in his home.
Then, a few months later,
she was sent to Philadelphia.
American soldiers
were supposed to be paid $6.67 a month.
But Congress had no money to pay them.
Most of the soldiers
went on fighting without pay.
Some refused to fight.
Instead, they took over the State House.

Congress had to move
to Princeton, New Jersey.
Deborah was sent to Philadelphia
with 1,500 other soldiers
to quiet the angry men.

Winter came.

Deborah's shoes were worn-out.

The army didn't give clothes to soldiers.

The men had to buy their own.

Deborah didn't have enough money
to buy new shoes.

Her bloody feet
left red stains in the snow.

Soon she became ill.

Once more, soldiers took her
to a hospital.
This time Deborah slept for days.
The doctors thought she was dead.
She could hear people
planning to bury her,
but she was too weak to cry out.
When a nurse passed by,
Deborah tried to groan.
The nurse heard her and ran for help.
Dr. Binney took Deborah's pulse.
He couldn't feel anything.
He reached under her shirt
to feel her heart.
The cloth tied around her chest
was in the way.
Dr. Binney ripped it off.

He stared in surprise.
There was no doubt about it.
Private Shurtleff was a woman!

Dr. Binney kept Deborah's secret,
but he decided that an army hospital
was no place for a woman.
He took Deborah home
to stay with his family.
Deborah still wore her army uniform.
Dr. Binney's family never knew
that she was a woman.

When she was well,

Deborah went back to her regiment.

The Revolutionary War

was coming to an end.

In 1783

Deborah was called to West Point.

Peace had been made.

The Americans had won!

Deborah's regiment

was no longer needed.

When she got to West Point,

General Paterson sent for Deborah.

He looked at a letter on his desk.

The letter was from Dr. Binney.

General Paterson laughed.

There *couldn't* be a woman in *my* army,
he thought.

The general showed the letter
to Deborah.

He thought that she would laugh too.

Instead, her face turned red.

General Paterson stared at her.

"Private Shurtleff," he said,

"I must ask this question.

Are you a woman?"

"Yes, sir," Deborah answered. "I am.

My real name is Deborah Sampson."

# What Happened Afterward?

Deborah Sampson was honorably discharged from the army on October 23, 1783. She returned to Massachusetts, where she stayed with her uncle who lived in Sharon. A young man named Benjamin Gannett lived nearby. The two fell in love and were married in April, 1784. They had three children: Earl, Mary, and Patience. They also adopted a fourth child, Susannah Shepherd. Susannah's mother had died in childbirth, and her father couldn't take care of her by himself.

Deborah and Benjamin's farm didn't do very well. They needed money, so Deborah earned some by giving speeches. She put on her army uniform and went on tour. Deborah Sampson was the first woman lecturer in the United States. She spoke about her Revolutionary War experiences, of course.

Deborah received $95 in army back pay from the Massachusetts Senate. Paul Revere helped her get a federal pension of $8 a month because she'd been wounded.

Deborah Sampson died in 1827 and was buried in Sharon, Massachusetts. The back of her tombstone reads, "Deborah Sampson Gannett, Robert Shurtleff, The Female Soldier. Service 1781-1783."